Hearts

Hearts

Poems by

Joanne Corey

Cover design by Shay Culligan
Cover photo by Brian Breeden on Unsplash
Author photo by Brent Boisvert

ISBN: 978-1-63980-347-7

Kelsay Books
502 South 1040 East, A-119
American Fork, Utah 84003
Kelsaybooks.com

for my parents

Acknowledgments

Many thanks to:

Karen Kelsay, Delisa Hargrove, and the whole team at Kelsay Books

The Binghamton Poetry Project, whose workshop prompts gave birth to several of these poems

My poet-friends from the Grapevine Poets and the Boiler House Poets Collective for their help in workshopping individual poems and this manuscript and for their advice and support

Tara Betts, Abby Murray, and Kyle Laws for making time in their busy lives to read *Hearts* and for their beautiful reflections

My sisters, Kathy and Karen

My spouse, Brent, and daughters, Beth and Trinity

My parents, Leo and Elinor Corey, for decades of love and support. Their loss is felt deeply by their family and many friends.

Prior Publications:

Spring 2017 Binghamton Poetry Project anthology: earlier versions of "Two Hearts" and "Waiting for Test Results"

In Transition: An Anthology of Womxn's Poetry, Ann Davenport, editor: "Sixteen Hours"

Spring 2021 Binghamton Poetry Project online anthology: "Over Eighty Years"

Contents

Discovery

I.

in late May heat
I mow near the back fence
stop to check the heirloom rose
transplanted shoot from my mother's garden

more wild than cultivated
her rose had first flourished
near her childhood home
moved with her many times
finally grown so large
it would not move
when the last house sold

the daughter rose
struggled in my backyard
assaulted by beetles
summer drought
this last dry, windy winter
without the protection of snow
when its lone cane snapped —
a late frost withered its few
remaining leaves

the joy of finding two new branches
springing from the broken stem —
a foot away
outside the bed
a new daughter rising
lush and green
already eight inches high —
a testament to strong roots

II.

The next year in June
rose-month
twin buds open

my mother bends over them
breathing in the memories of eight decades:
childhood, marriage, moves
parents, children, grandchildren
lean years, green years

III.

May rains
strengthen the heirloom rose
new shoots
spring-green
buds erupt
amid thorns

I pray beetles
don't attack
that there are no
hailstorms, no
accidents with
a lawn mower
so I may carry
roses to my mother's
sickroom, their fragrance
reaching her
despite the cannula
delivering oxygen

First Grandchild

When she arrived early,
you cuddled her,
light as a sack of sugar-and-spice
in your arms.

You diapered her,
snapped her into too-large sleepers,
rocked her,
hummed lullabies,
laid her in the same
white wicker bassinet
that had sheltered me
twenty-five years before.

You made soup,
washed clothes,
ironed them because
that was your way,
baked snickerdoodles,
kept vigil so I could catch
naps between ten daily feedings.

My tired eyes saw you:
grandmother-mother-daughter.
My heart expanded
as mother-daughter.
Our love lay swaddled
in the living room.

Two Hearts

Mom's cardiac rehab is Tuesday and Thursday mornings.

Dad rides with her in the retirement home van,
helps her navigate into the lift with her walker,
sits with her in the waiting room
until she is called into therapy
where he is not allowed to follow.

He waits.

Her exercises accomplished,
they board the van for the ride
back home to their apartment
where lunch awaits.

After sixty-two years of marriage,
he does not want her to go
alone.

Pharmacopia

The doctor said
reduce the diuretic
from two 20s
to one 10, one 20

and if blood
pressure drops
too low
or pulse races
too fast,
be careful standing
to avoid
dizziness.

Add a pill,
a dose so low
it's measured in micros.

Resume blood
thinner tonight.

Try not to forget to empty
each pillbox compartment —
breakfast — lunch — dinner — bedtime
each day of the week.

Try not to fall.

Try not to bleed.

A Condition of the Heart

From the other end
of the couch,
my mother
takes four breaths
to my one,
her heart
uncoordinated,
right chambers
enlarged
work fiercely
to force blood
through her mitral
valve, only to have
a share of it leak
back,
more and more
uncontrolled

At Night

In darkness, my heart
pounds too fast against
my ribs, blood throbs loud
in my ears, as though the umbilical
had never been severed.

Shopping List

We sit in silence
as you eat a few
spoonfuls of applesauce.

Dreading the unfamiliar
rasp in your voice,
I ask more questions
about the shopping list,
trying to intuit
what might entice
your failing appetite
and altered taste.

You like hummus
but crackers are now too sweet,
carrots too hard to chew.
Maybe a small zucchini
or peppers,
although they have to be yellow or red.
You can't tolerate green.

You have enough applesauce.

Almond butter
without sugar or salt

Some shortbreads in case you feel like a cookie

We discuss eating snacks throughout the day,
eating more in the morning and afternoon.
A dinner plate of food
in the evening
is too daunting.

Strawberry nutrition shakes

Six slices of American cheese from the deli

Tapioca pudding?
We settle on a six-pack of small
containers of rice pudding.
Pudding is a good idea.
You hadn't thought of that.

You shuffle from the chair to the couch
with your walker,
your shirt hanging
too large from your shoulders,
your heart not quite
keeping up.

I drive to the store
wondering if
this is a good day to live
or a good day to die.

Anamnesis

I surprise you with
mocha sauce from the
Apothecary Hall recipe.
Remembrances cascade
over coffee ice cream.

Waiting for Test Results

Her breaths come fast
and shallow between coughs.
I untie her sneakers,
work them off,

pull off her socks,
help her out of shirt and pants,
slip her nightgown on,
as she had done for me

when I was six,
speckled and feverish
with German measles
before there was a vaccine.

She sits on the edge
of the bed,
pivots to lie down,
needs me to lift

her feet.
The next day, she is isolated
in the hospital
with flu and pneumonia.

Care x2

My father lowers himself to a chair,
        red-faced,

shirt unbuttoned
        halfway,

exposing his T-shirt and alarm
        pendant.

The thermostat reads seventy-nine
        degrees.

He forgot to eat
        his lunch,

as he alternates between
        tending

to the laundry and
        helping

Mom get washed and
        dressed.

With Mom now clothed in
        layers,

I switch the thermostat
        to cool,

make sure
      he eats,

drinks some
      iced tea.

He buttons
      his shirt.

Sixteen Hours

Her doctor says it's time
to plan for end of life.
Hearts break. Tears flow.
Her granddaughter's water breaks.
Wide-eyed girl emerges. Tears flow.

Lemon Pizzelles

I. Pressing Time

A batch takes only thirty minutes
when we work as a team.
While the griddle heats,
my husband creams eggs and sugar,
as I melt a stick of butter.
He measures a cup and three-quarters flour
into the sifter, while I intersperse
two teaspoons baking powder.

By the time the press
is hot, the stiff batter is ready
for him to spoon slightly north of center
on each of the pair of designs.

He lowers and locks the lid.
I press the timer set for thirty seconds.
When it rings, I silence it
as he unlocks the press,
lifts the hot pizzelles onto the small
cooling rack I hold,
and spoons the next batch.
I move the cookies to a larger rack
as they stiffen,
stack when they are cool enough.

***

Spoon, press, timer, rack,
time divided into thirty-second increments
until the bowl is empty
and the tin full of pizzelles
to bring to my mother.
She shares a few with my father.

II. Marking Time

A friend says the women in her Italian neighborhood
used to time pizzelles by praying Hail Marys,
but disagreed on how many it took.
  Hail Mary, full of grace, the Lord is with thee . . .

When we called in hospice, your appetite was failing,
your tastes were changing.
You didn't want anything too sweet.
Lemon pizzelles, a favorite we made at Christmas, were perfect.
It was summer, but no reason now to wait.

It depends how fast you pray.
And in which language.
Latin would be faster. Fewer words.
  Ave Maria, gratia plena, Dominus tecum . . .
Or maybe they used Italian.
  Ave Maria, piena di grazia, il Signore è con te . . .

You say you like them because they are light. We agree,
smiling, knowing how much butter, how many eggs
go into each batch.

  . . . Blessed art thou amongst women,
  and blessed is the fruit of thy womb, Jesus.
  Holy Mary, Mother of God,
  pray for us sinners,
  now and at the hour of our death. Amen.

You eat lemon pizzelles every day, sometimes several times a day.
We make a new batch whenever you near the bottom of the tin.
We try other treats, but you always want your pizzelles, too.

Hail Mary, full of grace, the Lord is with thee.
Blessed art thou amongst women,
and blessed is the fruit of thy womb, Jesus.
Holy Mary, Mother of God,
pray for us sinners . . .

The pizzelles seem to help your appetite. We think you haven't lost
any more weight. One of the things about hospice is that you don't
have to do anything you don't want to.
You don't want to weigh yourself.

***

The bowl is almost empty.
Only one spoonful left for the last press.
One for Dad.

. . . now and at the hour of our death. Amen.
Hail Mary, full of grace, the Lord is with thee . . .

It depends how fast you pray.

Heirloom

Delicate white dress,
rising from the cedar chest,
clothes your great-grandchild,
your christening blessing.
Confined to home, you pray and wait.

Goodwill Ambassador

She'd make the rounds after dinner
in the community dining room,
asking about a spouse's health
or their granddaughter's graduation
or when they were flying out
to visit their son on the West Coast,
introducing herself to new residents,
always listening attentively
to the answers, remembering
each person's name and story.

Now, when I walk the halls
to their apartment, people stop
me to ask how Mom is doing,
tell me she was the first person
they met after they moved in,
how much they love her,
how sometimes, in her absence,
one or another of them
will go from table to table
visiting after dinner,
saying "I'm being Elinor today."

September Omen

The next item pencilled on the list
in my father's careful block letters:
"Kashi Organic Warm Cinnamon Cereal — 12 oz"

Because my mother always has a baggie
of them on her bed for nighttime snacking,
I easily find the box with its photo of oat hearts
mixed among the usual Os.

As I place it in the cart,
I notice the expiration
date, May 16, 2018:
her 86th birthday.

At Four Months

Your great-granddaughter doubles
her birthweight, brings hands
together, grasps her toes.
Too weak to hold her, you watch,
reach out to stroke her face.

Room 233

We've tried to make it seem
like home, your favorite
photos and prints and needlework
framed
on the institutional white

and a calendar with photos
of your great-grandchild
hanging over the board
where we write the date
every day, to remind
you which year
which month
which day
you have reached

February now
and we don't know
how many more pages
we will get to turn

Surely, we will be granted
March and your husband's
ninety-fourth birthday

Perhaps, April
and your 65th wedding
anniversary

But your May birthday
might be beyond
your reach

The room
someone else's
by then

On days

when you cry   salt   stains from
   re mem ber   lenses be fore
      to wash   vis it

Some Time Else

You wake from a nap
and look at the clock
which reads 10:35.
"I'm late for school."

"It's okay," I say, trying
to sound calm and reassuring.

You knit your brow
as you reassess the clock
face trying to make sense
of it. "Are you sure I'm not
late for school?"

"Yes, everything is fine.
You graduated."
You look relieved
and laugh
and smile as you drift
back into sleep.

Crying before the bathroom mirror,
I glimpse your mother,
seeing what you must have seen
in my tired eyes.

I'm grateful I had the presence
of mind not to call you "Mom."

Over Eighty Years

The scent of the white bells rings heavy
like when my child-self sat in the lily patch
near the barbed wire fence
submerged in the late afternoon valley darkness,

like your last May birthday
when we brought you
a nosegay of those same
flowers, a few pips

dug from the hemlock
humus that begat more
and more with wild
abandon to comfort

you
in your
last
May-days.

The hospice manual explains the signs of the last days

appetite fades
limbs weaken
drowsiness overwhelms
hands cool
sight darkens
skin mottles
breath slows

the sense of hearing heightens

As you lie motionless,
you hear your daughter,
or perhaps your long-dead
mother, singing you home.

About the Author

Joanne Corey re-discovered her childhood love of writing poetry in her fifties. She currently lives in Vestal, New York, where she participates with the Binghamton Poetry Project, Broome County Arts Council, Tioga Arts Council, and Grapevine Poets. With the Boiler House Poets Collective, she has completed an (almost) annual residency week at the Massachusetts Museum of Contemporary Art in North Adams since 2015. Her work has appeared in *Wilderness House Literary Review, Rat's Ass Review,* and *Third Wednesday Magazine,* among others, and in several online series with Silver Birch Press and *The Ekphrastic Review* Writing Challenges, as well as in anthologies with QuillsEdge Press, GWL Publishing (UK), University Professors Press, and the Binghamton Poetry Project. She was featured poet in the December 2022 edition of *Portrait of New England. Hearts* is her first book.

She invites you to visit her eclectic blog at
topofjcsmind.wordpress.com.